A SELF-LOVE, I-AM-AMAZING, WORKBOOK AND GUIDED JOURNAL DESIGNED FOR AMAZING PEOPLE

LEAVE THAT JUNK BEHIND

A Self-Love Workbook For Replacing Negative Thoughts, Re-Building Self-Esteem, and Taking Your Life Back!

ALEXIS CARTER, MA

Keep Your Hands
Off My Book

_____

_____

This book is dedicated to
everyone who is tired of the
crap and needs a chance
to re-center themselves
with compassion and love.

I know how hard it can
sometimes be, and I salute you.

Contents

Introduction

HELLO AND WELCOME!

First of all, congratulations on carving out some much-needed time out of your insanely busy life to dedicate solely to…. yourself!

We are tough. We do it all. We manage it all. We take care of it all. We bear it all.

We are also the first to criticize ourselves and the last to pat ourselves on the back for an excellent job well done. I am here to pat you on your back and remind you that you are formidable and capable of anything you put your mind to.

Most people I meet could run an entire city with the energy they spend on being critical and negative toward themselves. (Myself included at times.)

I often wonder:

- Why do we do this to ourselves?
- Why do we look for faults in others to feel better about our own lives and bodies?
- Why do negative thoughts so often pop into our heads before any positive and motivating ones?
- Why are we surprised when someone tells us we are beautiful, intelligent, and capable?
- Why do we forget to care for ourselves and then wonder why we are slowly losing our damn minds?
- Why do we give fantastic, loving advice to others and immediately fail to apply it to ourselves?

These questions are always on my mind after I meet beautiful, capable, bright people who genuinely think they are unattractive, incompetent, dumb, or poor parents. Men and women constantly short-change themselves, see deficiencies where others see strengths, and see ugliness where others see beauty. Well....listen up, my friend. We are going to change that, starting with YOU!

This workbook developed as I wrote Stop Being a Doormat and Learn to Love Yourself. I wanted a companion workbook that incorporated the concepts and lessons included in the book and provided ready-made exercises and activities to help you reflect on what is eating at you, take the negative thoughts you employed during the day and process them differently, and finally, how to appreciate yourself the way you deserve.

When we constantly repeat a critical, self-deprecating, internal narrative about who we think we are and how others perceive us, we create real pathways in our brains that keep chugging along on this destructive ride until we tell them to STOP.

Our brains are amazing organs. They are our protectors, and they love learning and improving. We are going to train yours to go for the positive and loving pathway first. This will enable you to practice self-love and compassion, see yourself for the incredible woman you are, and learn to give yourself a damn break!

Inside, you will find guided journals and cognitive and dialectical behavioral exercises to help you:

- Observe and analyze your daily thoughts and behaviors.
- Rebuild and strengthen your self-esteem.
- Learn how creativity is a fun and easy way to practice relaxation, mindfulness, and re-center.
- Learn to be aware of negative thoughts and stop them before they take root.
- Improve self-compassion and confidence, and learn to embrace everything you are.

With practice, repetition, and a bit of blunt humor, you will take back your life and be the amazing person you have always wanted to be!

Let's get started!

X

CHAPTER 1
What are Negative Narratives and
Why You Need to Ditch Yours

Negative narratives come from that mean, hyper-critical personal critic that lives in your brain. They are always right there, playing on a loop in your head.

These critics are highly trained because you do a great job of reinforcing them by allowing them to interfere and BELIEVING what they say! The more often you do something, the easier a habit forms and is tougher to kick.

It doesn't help that the brain hormone Dopamine, the happy, feel good-hormone, gives you a little burst when you are both happy and sad. So when your critic pipes up with a negative thought, you feel sad and upset, and dopamine jumps in to make you feel better. Your negative narrative is now rewarded and reinforced again.

Don't fret, you can control this, and we will review how you can break this nasty habit.

I'm just not smart enough.

I can never do it right.

I'll never get a promotion.

No one wants to date me.

Why am I so fat?

He is better than me.

Why can't I ever get a break?

My Personal Negative Critic who Lives in My Brain

Pull out your pens and pencils, and unleash the negative thoughts you like to give time and attention to. I have provided you with a negative narrative phrase to get you started. Go ahead and answer it with the negative responses that pop into your mind. Or create a negative phrase and response you know you tend to repeat.

THIS SITUATION OR PEOPLE ANNOYED ME THE MOST TODAY:

Example Answer: The chaotic team meeting really annoyed me

_____

_____

_____

I GOT ANGRY TODAY WHEN::

_____

_____

_____

_____

THE WORST THOUGHTS I HAD TODAY WERE:

_____

_____

_____

_____

I SPENT TOO MUCH TIME WORRYING ABOUT:

_____

_____

_____

_____

AND THERE IS MORE, KEEP THE IDEAS FLOWING...

Either take a break, or stay on a roll, and keep leaving those negative thoughts behind.

I WISH I WASN'T SO BAD AT:

_____

_____

_____

_____

I AM OVERLOOKED AT WORK BECAUSE:

_____

_____

_____

_____

I WISH I DIDN'T HAVE THIS PROBLEM:

_____

_____

_____

_____

I HAVE NO CONTROL OVER:

_____

_____

_____

_____

KEEP GOING!

Now, add additional negative thoughts you regularly have which may have come to mind from the exercise. If you don't have any more right now, that's fine. Come back to it later when the thought creeps in. It is critical to start identifying these habitual negative thought patterns and learn to interrupt them before they take hold. You can use this page as you need to.

LET'S REPHRASE AND RE-TRAIN OUR BRAINS

Here, take the response you provided to each of the negative phrases. Show how to continue the thought by re-phrasing the negative reaction with a followup alternative compassionate narrative.

THIS REALLY ANNOYED ME:

EXAMPLE: The chaotic team meeting reallly annoyed me, but I handled it well by remaining calm and professional.

_____

_____

_____

_____

I GOT ANGRY TODAY WHEN:

_____

_____

_____

_____

THE WORST THOUGHT I HAD TODAY WAS:

_____

_____

_____

_____

I SPENT TOO MUCH TIME WORRYING ABOUT:

_____

_____

_____

_____

GAIN CONTROL OVER YOUR THOUGHTS

When you catch yourself rigidly thinking with "I always, or I never phrase," try and rephrase them into a more open response similar to I chose to do this, I can do anything I like, I can choose to be upset or let it go. Actively saying what you choose to do is freeing and gives a sense of control.

I WISH I WEREN'T SO BAD AT:

_____

_____

_____

_____

I AM OVERLOOKED AT WORK BECAUSE:

_____

_____

_____

_____

I WISH I DIDN'T HAVE THIS PROBLEM:

_____

_____

_____

_____

I HAVE NO CONTROL OVER:

_____

_____

_____

_____

THIS TAKES PRACTICE, BE PATIENT

Unlearning an ingrained, negative thought pattern takes time and effort. Suppose you've thought this way for many years. In that case, it will require active repetition and a conscious effort to distance yourself from the automatic negative responses and to rephrase with a more loving and positive phrase.

_____

_____

_____

_____

_____

_____

_____

_____

_____

_____

_____

_____

_____

_____

IT WILL BECOME MORE NATURAL OVER TIME

Repeatedly exposing yourself to positive narrations and visualizations will naturally lead to thinking about them automatically. Start by telling yourself you are making the choices. This cognitive habit will be easier as you free your mind and control your own rules and script. This space is for any additional journaling you would like to do.

Instead of...
Changing the Narrative

Behaviors change only after our THOUGHTS change. Changing your thinking will positively direct how you act and see yourself. With repetition, this will become your new thought and behavioral patterns because you have ingrained a new narrative. Use this exercise to re-train your habitual negative thoughts into self-esteem and self-love-building responses.

INSTEAD OF THIS	SAY THIS
I just got lucky	I worked hard for this and deserve it

CHAPTER 2
Self-Esteem to the Rescue

Self-esteem is how you value and see yourself. It can influence your motivation, life choices, mental well-being, and overall quality of life.

It also has to do with a perceived sense of worthiness or unworthiness.

A negative self-perception can quickly derail you and cause depression, anxiety, low self-confidence and other health problems..

Key elements to self-esteem include:

- Self-confidence
- Feelings of security
- A strong sense of self
- Sense of belonging
- Feeling of competence

Ways to improve low self-esteem

- Recognize what you're good at.
- Build positive relationships.
- Be kind to yourself.
- Learn to be assertive.
- Start saying "no" without regret.
- Give yourself a new challenge.

SELF-ESTEEM QUIZ

GOOD SELF ESTEEM HELPS YOU TO HAVE:

A. CONFIDENCE   C. MOOD SWINGS
B. OPTIMISM   D   BOTH A & B

HAVING A POSITIVE ATTITUDE TOWARD YOUR FUTURE, MEANS YOU ARE:

A. RESILIENT   C. OPTIMISTIC
B. CONFIDENT   D   ALL OF THE ABOVE

SELF-AWARENESS INCLUDES KNOWING ABOUT MY...

A. STRENGTHS   C. PERSONAL HOBBIES
B. WEAKNESSES   D   ALL OF THE ABOVE

WHAT IS A "NEED"?

A. A BOAT   C. CLOTHES
B. FLOWERS   D   FOOD

Answers: ALL D

ASSESS WHERE YOU ARE NOW

Before we begin, I suggest you understand your self-esteem levels. Self-awareness of our moods, state of mind, and attitudes are crucial to moving forward in a healthy direction.

How will you rate the following

PHYSICAL		Never	Rarely	Sometimes	Always
	I feel good about my body	○	○	○	○
	I exercise to keep my body healthy	○	○	○	○
	I get 7-8 hours of sleep every	○	○	○	○
	night	○	○	○	○
	I include nutritious food in my diet	○	○	○	○
	I smoke				

How will you rate the following

EMOTIONAL		Never	Rarely	Sometimes	Always
	I can manage my feelings properly	○	○	○	○
	I can cope when stressed	○	○	○	○
	I have a positive outlook and energy	○	○	○	○
	I allot time for my interests	○	○	○	○

SELF-ESTEEM JOURNAL

Here are two weeks of guided journaling to get you started. I encourage you to continue this on your own once it's completed.

MON	Something I did well today... Today I had fun when... I felt happy when...
TUE	Today I accomplished... I had a positive experience with... I made a difference when...
WED	I felt good about myself when... I was proud of myself when... Today was interesting because...
THU	What does feeling self-assured mean to you? Who are the people that improve your life? I felt proud when...
FRI	I overcame this today... This is my favorite part of my body... I am really skilled in...
SAT	I am looking forward to... I have overcome this fear... I am grateful for...
SUN	These are my three favorite qualities about yourself? These are three qualities that you hope to possess? This was the best moment of my day or week...

Extra Space for thoughts

SELF-ESTEEM JOURNAL

Week 2

MON	I felt great about myself when... I decided not to get frustrated when... I have learned to care about...
TUE	This was a personal success today... I caught myself being negative when... I made a positive impact when...
WED	My close friends are... I achieved this today... My best feature is....
THU	What does feeling self-assured mean to you? Who are the people that improve your life? I do this very well...
FRI	This made me feel powerful... I am optimistic about... This will be a great personal achievement...
SAT	Self-assured mean this to me... I have overcome this self-doubt... I am grateful for...
SUN	I need to repeat this to help stay positive about myself... I showed self-compassion when... This was the highlight of my week...

Extra Space for thoughts

5 MINUTE SELF-ESTEEM GUIDED JOURNAL

I EXCEL AT:

_____

_____

_____

_____

THESE ARE THREE GOOD THINGS ABOUT ME:

_____

_____

_____

_____

I OVERCAME THIS CHALLENGE:

_____

_____

_____

_____

5 MINUTE SELF-ESTEEM
GUIDED JOURNAL

I AM DOING THIS TO SHOW SELF-CARE AND LOVE:

_____

_____

_____

_____

I AM AWARE OF THESE NEGATIVE THOUGHT PATTERNS:

_____

_____

_____

_____

I AM OVERCOMING THIS SELF-DOUBT:

_____

_____

_____

_____

SELF-ESTEEM BINGO

This is your own BINGO game to complete at your leisure.
Mark off items as you accomplish them. When you achieve a
BINGO, treat yourself to something amazing.

MASTER A NEW SKILL	LET NEGATIVE PEOPLE GO	STAND AT THE EDGE OF COMFORT ZONE	DO SOMETHING CREATIVE OFTEN	AFFIRM YOURSELF OFTEN
EXPRESS FEELINGS	ACCEPT FAILURES AS PART OF GROWTH	OVERCOME A FEAR	MANAGE STRESS	MAKE TIME FOR FRIENDS
EXERCISE OFTEN	CULTIVATE HOBBIES	LOVE ME	LIVE HUMBLY	BE KIND TO YOURSELF
HONOR YOUR WORD TO OTHERS	REMIND YOURSELF YOU ARE ENOUGH	LOVE YOURSELF MORE THAN OTHERS WILL	DREAM BIG AND MAKE IT HAPPEN	CHALLENGE LIMITING BELIEFS
HELP SOMEONE	STOP WORRYING ABOUT WHAT OTHERS THINK	WALK AWAY FROM TOXICITY	READ SOMETHING INSPIRATIONAL	RECLAIM INTEGRITY

4 EASY WAYS TO DISPLAY CONFIDENCE TO OTHERS

Eye Contact- Always

Keeping eye contact with someone shows respect and demonstrates a sense of self-confidence, even if you don't actually feel it.

Smile (Even if you don't feel it)

You will appear more confident and comfortable to everyone when you are relaxed and smiling.

Body Positioning

Keep your head up, increase your stride, smile and make eye contact with a few people.

Believe You are a Badass

If you believe you are capable, beautiful, and self-assured then you unconsciously will appear that way to everyone all the time.

CHAPTER 3
Know Your Values and Strengths and What You Can Control

The more familiar you are with your natural strengths, the more you can draw from them to discover and identify new opportunities to improve them.

When you know where you excel and what you have to offer, you feel confident, capable, and self-assured as you move through life.

Identifying values is another critical step to improving self-esteem and self-confidence.

We naturally gravitate to like-minded people who continue reinforcing the best in us.

When we know who we are, we feel more stable and optimistic about our futures..

Fighting against what we can't control is pointless and a definite way to drive yourself crazy and cause depression and anxiety.

When stressed, identify what is realistically within your control and focus on what you can do to improve the situation.

PERSONAL VALUES

Pick any 5 core values that you hold in high esteem

LOVE	HONESTY
WEALTH	LOYALTY
FAMILY	REASON
MORALS	BEAUTY
KNOWLEDGE	PEACE
POWER	WISDOM
ADVENTURE	RELAXATION
POPULARITY	SAFETY

PERSONAL VALUES RANKING

Our values shape us and define us. Please use the top 5 values from page 22 and rank them in order of preference. Write what the value means to you.

Consider your values and others you may want to explore further.

_____

_____

_____

_____

_____

_____

_____

_____

_____

_____

_____

_____

_____

_____

_____

Strength Exploration Checklist
Strike off items you feel you are very good at

- [ ] I am very capable and intelligent.

- [ ] I am honest with my friends and family.

- [ ] I am open-minded and non-judgemental.

- [ ] I am empathetic to other people's pain.

- [ ] I have a love for learning.

- [ ] I am kind and compassionate.

- [ ] I have a good sense of humor.

- [ ] I am optimistic in my approach toward life.

- [ ] I am humble with my achievements.

- [ ] I am assertive with people.

Continue to think of strengths you have and new ones you would like to develop

_____

_____

_____

_____

_____

_____

_____

_____

_____

_____

_____

_____

_____

_____

_____

_____

Circle of Control

Many things are in your control, but many are not. This exercise allows you to reflect upon items that are reasonably in your circle of control.

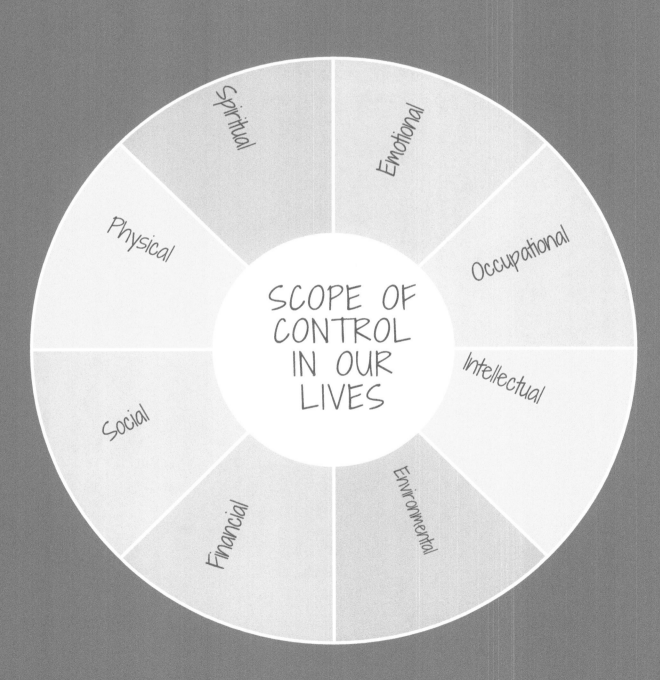

Think of issues that are causing you anxiety, depression, or stress. Which issues are in your control? Which are not?

Inside this circle, add issues that are IN YOUR CONTROL and leave the other problems that are NOT IN YOUR CONTROL outside the circle.

For example,
Inside: "Worrying about finishing a 5k race" (because only you can control how much you train for it).
Outside: "Worrying about getting the promotion" (because you cannot control what others decide, so worrying is a waste of your time).

Continue to think of troubling issues you have and determine if they are in your control.

_____

_____

_____

_____

_____

_____

_____

_____

_____

_____

_____

_____

_____

_____

_____

_____

CHAPTER 4
Self-Love and Self-Care

Self-love is:

- Confident, generous, caring, and unconditional.
- It does not judge.
- It is a total acceptance of who and what you are.
- It empowers us to say no to dysfunctional people.
- It pushes us to new levels of success.

Self-love is the self-care and compassion you give yourself, which paves the way to improved self-esteem, increased peace and happiness, and enhanced mental health.

Evidence-based benefits of loving yourself:

- Better mental health.
- Increased happiness.
- Improved self-esteem.
- Increased motivation.
- More drive and passion.
- Increased self-awareness.
- Less stress and anxiety.
- Better sleep

Self-care is taking the time to attend to your physical, mental, and emotional health. It drives you to achieve goals and improve the quality of your life.

.

Self-care helps you effectively manage stress, anxiety, and depression and achieve a balanced state of mind.

Self-Love Checklist
Strike off items you agree with.

- [ ] .I love everything about myself.
- [ ] I know that some social expectations are not realistic.
- [ ] I know that I can't control everything.
- [ ] I am forgiving of my mistakes.
- [ ] I manage my stress and emotions well.
- [ ] I am kind and compassionate to myself.
- [ ] I do not need approval from others to feel good about myself.
- [ ] I do not stay in toxic relationships.
- [ ] I love to take care of my body and stay healthy.
- [ ] I know who I am and I am comfortable in my own skin..

Use this space to reflect on the items you did not choose and why?

_____

_____

_____

_____

_____

_____

_____

_____

_____

_____

_____

_____

_____

_____

SELF-CARE ASSESSMENT

Think of your average week or month. How often do you accomplish these common self-care activities? Check up to 5 times

1. 2. 3. 4. 5. **Psychological/Emotional Self-Care**

☐☐☐☐☐ Participate in hobbies

☐☐☐☐☐ Go on vacations or day-trips

☐☐☐☐☐ Find reasons to laugh

☐☐☐☐☐ Talk about my problems

☐☐☐☐☐ Find a creative outlet to relax with

1. 2. 3. ★ **Social Self-Care**

☐☐☐ ☐ Spend time with people who I like

☐☐☐ ☐ Meet new people

☐☐☐ ☐ Initiate or participate in fun outings with others

☐☐☐ ☐ Keep in touch with old friends

☐☐☐ ☐ Ask others for help, when needed

10 SELF-CARE Activites

1. Go outside for a daily walk

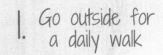

2. Journal every morning

3. Spend more time with family & friends

4. Take time to indulge in some pampering

5. Declutter your home

6. Practice positive affirmations

7. Get more sleep every night

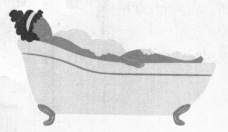

8. Read more books

10. Schedule time for daily meditation

9. Take up yoga or a different exercise

CHAPTER 5
Postive-Affirmations and Daily Gratitude

Positive affirmations are a potent, often overlooked tool to reprogram our negative thought patterns and the nasty critic living in our brains.

Our subconscious mind plays a significant role in helping us create the reality we want to achieve. Telling yourself an affirmation and envisioning it applying to your life teaches your subconscious mind to believe certain things about yourself.

Repeating daily affirmations significantly impacts the outcome of future events and new ingrained perceptions of yourself.

Positive affirmations help you see yourself in a positive light when you need a motivational boost.

When we feel confident and positive about ourselves, our lives are happier, and less stressful, and we are more apt to succeed.

Likewise, when we see ourselves negatively, we tend to engage in self-defeating behaviors, which may lead to negative outcomes.

Regularly assessing what you are grateful for is strongly associated with increased happiness, self-love, and self-esteem.

Gratitude helps you stay in a healthy frame of mind longer, be more mindful of positive experiences, improve your mental and physical health and become more optimistic.

You are also in a better mindset to overcome challenges and build solid relationships.

Daily Affirmations

This is an excellent page to tear out and cut into daily affirmations. Place them around your house, your mirror, your computer, your purse, or anywhere else you will frequently see them for a reminder.

I am confident and comfortable in my own skin

I am grateful for my life

I don't need anyone to validate me

I am freaking amazing

I am perfect the way I am

I have a beautiful mind and body

When I want something, I go for it

I don't allow others to bring me down

I am worthy. I am loved. I am enough.

I am resilient and can get through anything

I am beautiful, confident, and smart

I deserve love and kindness

DAILY AFFIRMATION AND
GRATITUDE JOURNAL

 S M T W T F S

DAILY POSITIVE AFFIRMATION	I AM GRATEFUL FOR

SELF-CARE PLANS FOR TODAY

- ---
- ---
- ---

I AM WORTHY BECAUSE:	TODAY I AM FEELING:

37

DAILY AFFIRMATION AND GRATITUDE JOURNAL

 S M T W T F S

DAILY POSITIVE AFFIRMATION	I AM GRATEFUL FOR

SELF-CARE PLANS FOR TODAY

- _____
- _____
- _____

I AM WORTHY BECAUSE:	TODAY I AM FEELING:

DAILY AFFIRMATION AND GRATITUDE JOURNAL

S M T W T F S

DAILY POSITIVE AFFIRMATION	I AM GRATEFUL FOR

SELF-CARE PLANS FOR TODAY

- _____
- _____
- _____

I AM WORTHY BECAUSE:	TODAY I AM FEELING:

39

DAILY AFFIRMATION AND
GRATITUDE JOURNAL

DAILY POSITIVE AFFIRMATION	I AM GRATEFUL FOR

SELF-CARE PLANS FOR TODAY

- _____
- _____
- _____

I AM WORTHY BECAUSE:	TODAY I AM FEELING:

DAILY AFFIRMATION AND GRATITUDE JOURNAL

DAILY POSITIVE AFFIRMATION	I AM GRATEFUL FOR

SELF-CARE PLANS FOR TODAY

- _____
- _____
- _____

I AM WORTHY BECAUSE:	TODAY I AM FEELING:

DAILY AFFIRMATION AND
GRATITUDE JOURNAL

DAILY POSITIVE AFFIRMATION	I AM GRATEFUL FOR

SELF-CARE PLANS FOR TODAY

-
-
-

I AM WORTHY BECAUSE:	TODAY I AM FEELING:

DAILY AFFIRMATION AND GRATITUDE JOURNAL

DAILY POSITIVE AFFIRMATION

I AM GRATEFUL FOR

SELF-CARE PLANS FOR TODAY

-
-
-

I AM WORTHY BECAUSE:

TODAY I AM FEELING:

CHAPTER 6
Break for Mindfulness

MINDFULNESS

Mindfulness is the practice of focusing on what you are doing at the present moment, of not being distracted by worries, stress, and anxious, irritating thoughts. To be mindful, slow down and take your time.

Mindfulness Practice

Before you roll your eyes and think I am suggesting that you find a dark, heated room, a yoga mat, and play some soothing Tibetian chants in the background, take a moment to understand what being Mindful means.

Current research has shown that increasing mindfulness can be as effective as anti-depressants and anti-anxiety medication in some individuals.

Mindfulness practices help you manage stress, cope more efficiently with illness, and reduce depression and anxiety.

Those who practice mindfulness report an increased ability to relax, generate greater enthusiasm for life and improve self-esteem and gratitude.

You also create room for self-love and self-care when you focus on yourself.

Three key characteristics of mindfulness:
- Intention to the act of staying aware and present, no wandering minds with stressful or distracting thoughts.
- Attention to what is occurring at that present moment (observing thoughts, feelings, and sensations).
- Maintaining a non-judgmental attitude and being compassionate and kind to yourself.

Mindfulness means being present or living in the moment and finding joy in simple pleasures.
It could be in a heated, dark yoga studio, but it also can be:
- Driving in your car, on autopilot, and listening to music.
- Going to a Farmer's Market and taking the time to visit each booth and experience the atmosphere, smells, and products.
- Eating your favorite food and savoring each bite.
- Holding your baby and giving her your full attention
- Engaging in creative activities like coloring or painting
All of these are examples you can be mindful, aware, and focused on one thing only.

Mindfulness Practice

What emotions am I feeling right now?	
What are these feelings trying to tell me?	
How is my body reacting?	
What am I thinking right now?	

12 Days of 3 Minute Mindfulness Activities

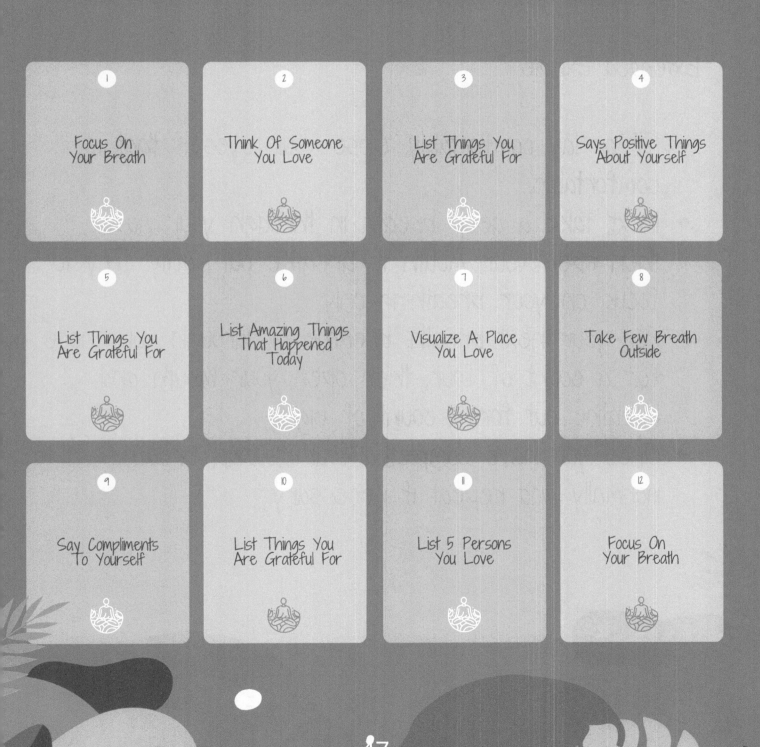

1 Focus On Your Breath	**2** Think Of Someone You Love	**3** List Things You Are Grateful For	**4** Says Positive Things About Yourself
5 List Things You Are Grateful For	**6** List Amazing Things That Happened Today	**7** Visualize A Place You Love	**8** Take Few Breath Outside
9 Say Compliments To Yourself	**10** List Things You Are Grateful For	**11** List 5 Persons You Love	**12** Focus On Your Breath

Mindfulness Meditation Breathing Practice

Try simple meditation exercises if you are struggling to give yourself time to yourself or need help unwinding and de-stressing.

Extended Exhale

- Sit or lay comfortably. Close your eyes if that is comfortable.
- Next, take a deep breath in through your nose, then open your mouth to breathe out softly. Try to focus on your breathing only.
- For your next breath, breathe in through your nose for a count of four, then open your mouth and breathe out for a count of eight.
- Once you have completed four rounds, breathe normally and repeat if necessary.

Mindfulness Practice

Focus on what you are grateful for when you are in the moment, not distracted by negative, stressful, or extraneous thoughts. When we focus on gratitude, we focus on ourselves and our self-worth.

Think of 8 things you are grateful for today.

1._____

2._____

3._____

45._____

—

6._____

7._____

8._____

5 minute journaling

CHAPTER 7
Relax and Color Already

Art and creative exercises have been proven to be highly effective mindfulness activities for relaxing and reducing stress and anxiety.
When you are balanced, you can work on self-care and self-esteem-building more effectively.

Next are several meditative coloring pages to give you a moment to unwind, de-stress, and take a damn break!

Grab your colored pencils, crayons, or markers, sit back, and zone out!

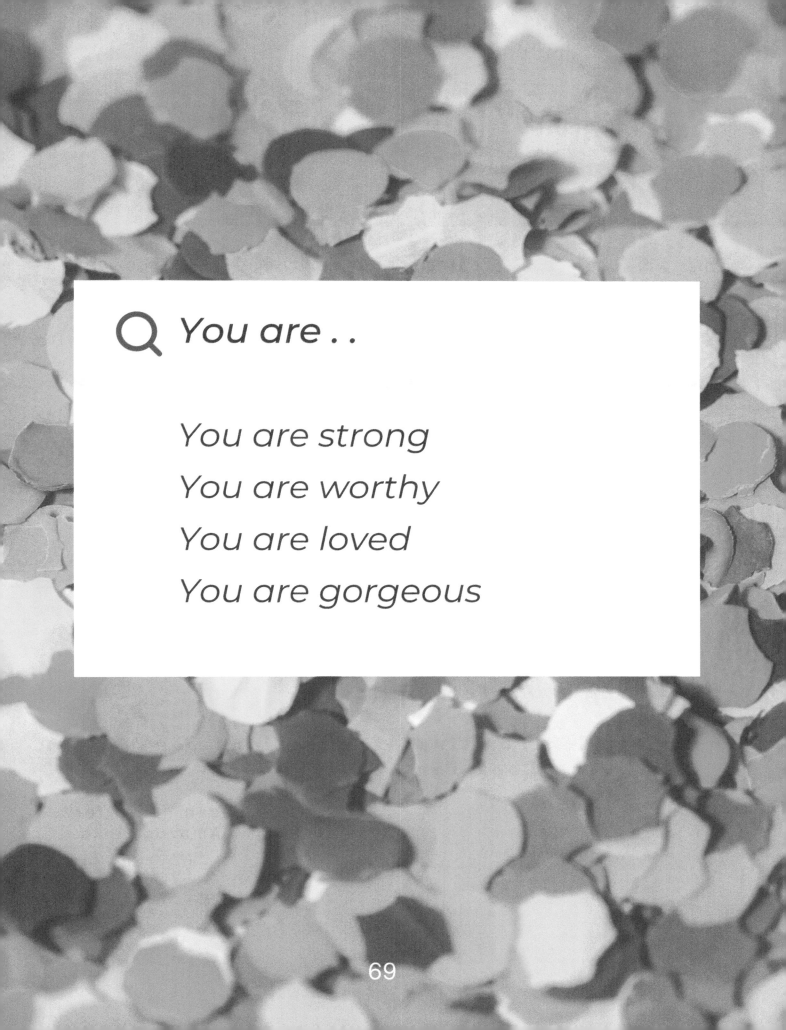

Q *You are . .*

You are strong

You are worthy

You are loved

You are gorgeous

Additional Resources

This workbook was created as an individual resource and as a supplement to the book:

Stop Being a Doormat and Learn to Love Yourself by Alexis Carter on Amazon.

If you would like to find out more about the coloring book pages that were included, please refer to the following titles by Alexis Carter on Amazon:

- *Relax with Flowers, A Coloring Book for Adults*

- *Relax with Animals, A Coloring Book for Adults*

- *Relax with Mindfulness Meditations, A Coloring Book for Adults*

- *Relax with Positive Affirmations for Women, A Coloring Book for Adults*

Scan Below for
Amazon Links

Additional Resources

If you have a teenage daughter, friend, sister, or niece that could benefit from a workbook for self-esteem, confidence, and body image, please be sure to look at the following on Amazon:

- **You've Got This Girl, a self-esteem workbook and journal for girls**

- **Relax with Motivational Quotes Coloring Book for Girls**

Scan Below for Amazon Links

About
THE AUTHOR

Alexis Carter has a master's degree and a specialty in behavioral psychology. Her expertise is in developing self-awareness, healthy relationship strategies, and identifying negative patterns and self-esteem issues that can lead to unwanted dysfunction in relationships and personal and professional lives.

Alexis's goal is to arm teens, men, and women with practical strategies and techniques to understand ingrained behaviors, develop healthy relationships, create realistic perspectives and priorities, and manage challenges and traumas that can affect personal success.

She has created many self-help books, workbooks, journals, and coloring books designed to address self-esteem, coping strategies, confidence building, stress management, and mindfulness.

Alexis is a busy single mom of twins and lives in Southern California with her children.

My Thanks

Dear Reader,

Thank you for giving yourself some individual time and completing this self-love workbook and journal. I am passionate about helping women achieve their best and truly enjoyed creating this workbook for you.

Many readers do not know how critical reviews are for an author and how difficult they are to come by.

I would be very grateful if you could write a brief review on Amazon. If you have suggestions for improvement or additional content, I encourage you to contact me directly at www.creativeworksbooks.com.

Thank you for sharing your thoughts, and I wish you all the best in your self-improvement journey.

Scan to Review

Warmest regards,

Alexis

Made in the USA
Las Vegas, NV
26 December 2023

83575730R00046